Penwith

IN OLD PHOTOGRAPHS

Penwith

IN OLD PHOTOGRAPHS

Compiled by JONATHAN HOLMES

Alan Sutton Publishing Limited
Phoenix Mill · Far Thrupp · Stroud
Gloucestershire

First published 1993

Copyright © Jonathan Holmes, 1993

British Library Cataloguing in Publication Data

Holmes, Jonathan
Penwith in Old Photographs
  I. Title
  942.375

ISBN 0-7509-0428-3

Typeset in 9/10 Sabon.
Typesetting and origination by
Alan Sutton Publishing Limited.
Printed in Great Britain by
Redwood Books, Trowbridge.

Contents

Introduction

Penwith is one of the ancient names for west Cornwall. It was the name of the old hundred, and has also been translated to mean 'the Land's End'. This volume is designed to give a flavour of life in the region over the last 100 or so years.

The area has great contrasts – from the wild rugged moors to the quiet valleys running down to tranquil coves. The north coast has some of the most spectacular cliff scenery to be seen in England. These contrasts can be seen in the variety of communities that dot the landscape from St Just to Zennor, from Sennen to St Ives.

People make history, not places. Their actions have shaped the landscape and buildings constructed from the local granite stand as reminders of the past. Among the harbours surrounding the coastline, the earliest date from around the thirteenth century, although there was already a seaborne trade in the Neolithic (or New Stone Age) period.

The area has one of the greatest concentrations of archaeological sites in Europe. The quoits, megaliths, stone circles and settlements show that mankind has lived in this landscape for thousands of years. How these monuments were constructed and what they were used for is still a matter for discussion and conjecture.

The arrival of the Christian religion at the beginning of the medieval period led to the construction of many churches, but all of them were rebuilt by the Victorians and they no longer resemble the early constructions. John and Charles Wesley visited the area and a change of worshipping habit took place; Nonconformist chapels sprang up in every village and hamlet. These were filled to capacity by god-fearing mining and fishing communities who had left the Church of England.

The custom of celebrating Midsummer was carried on in Penzance until the turn of this century. The Quay Fair, the burning of tar barrels and the lighting of bonfires along the sea-front have not been revived, although the Feast of Golowan (Feast of St John) has been, and with great success.

The rough coastline has been the graveyard of many a proud ship. The construction of lighthouses helped to stop such destruction, but many a vessel has found its way down to Davy Jones's locker. It is said that more vessels have been lost around the area's coastline than anywhere else in Britain.

Today the major industry of the district is tourism, but whether it should be seen as the mainstay of the economy is doubtful. Although tourists have flocked to Cornwall for over 150 years, the region may not be able compete with today's package tours to foreign destinations. Probably the most important local tourist destination is not Penzance or St Ives but the Land's End, which seems to have such a mystical fascination that thousands are drawn to it. The Land's End has been developed over the last 100 years to provide today's only all-weather attraction of any size.

Although the significance of tourism must not be underestimated, fishing, farming and horticulture are very important to the economy of the region. The once-thriving mining and quarrying industries no longer exist. The Geevor mine complex, which was purchased by Cornwall County Council for a heritage park, opened its doors for the first time this year, but it has yet to prove itself.

The photographs included in this volume have come from the collections of Penzance & District Museum & Art Gallery, the Penzance Library, Morrab Gardens and a number of private collections.

Jonathan J. Holmes
Curator of Penzance & District Museum & Art Gallery

SECTION ONE
People

The Maids of the Mill: the miller of Bosava Mill with his family. The mill was immortalized in Lamorna Birch's famous painting *January, the Mill at Lamorna*.

Evangeline Booth and the Salvation Army outside the Land's End Hotel in the 1930s.

Wesleyan tea treat on Treglown's Picnic Grounds, Marazion, 1908. Treglown's Picnic Grounds were situated in Marazion but were used and visited by people and groups from throughout Penwith.

Church parade in Pendeen. The banner reads, 'St John the Baptist Church, Pendeen'. It is difficult to date this view, but it is probably from just prior to the First World War.

Digging tank traps, Eastern Green beach, Penzance, in the early 1940s. Mount's Bay was an important staging point for the invasion of France and was therefore held to be a major target for enemy action.

This group of fishermen at the turn of the century has been identified as, left to right, Edgar Reynolds, William Harvey, -?-, William Simons and, front row, Willie

Harvey and Willie Bone.

East coast fishermen washing out their fish boxes under Tolcarne Bridge, Newlyn. The fishing year fell into seasons and it was usual for fishermen from other ports to work out of Newlyn at certain times.

The lady on the left is Phylis Yglesias, the founder of the Mousehole Bird Hospital. She treated many oiled and sick birds, and the hospital continues this important work today.

Ella Napper, a well-known jeweller, lived at Trewoofe, Lamorna. She is seen here working on a bone hair comb. The artist Dame Laura Knight was a great friend of hers and they worked together on at least one piece of enamel jewellery.

The wheelwright was an important member of any farming community, mending the farm carts and making wheels. At one time there were a large number of wheelwrights operating in the district; none survive today.

This delightful study of two young girls at a chute in Newlyn was taken by John Branwell, an amateur photographer, in the mid-1880s. Until mains water was available, collecting water from a chute or well was a daily chore.

A photograph taken in 1974 showing the last mayor of the Borough of Penzance, Councillor David Pooley, and his wife, holding the town's charter, which dates from 1614. In the centre is the town clerk Mr E.O. Wheale and on the right are the deputy mayor, Councillor John Laity, and his wife.

Lord St Levan's boatmen in ceremonial dress. They rowed the Mount's barge in this costume on special occasions such as the visit of Queen Victoria in 1846.

Dolly Pentreath is said to have been the last monoglot Cornish speaker. This has been challenged by many, but she has certainly earned her place in the history of the Cornish language.

SECTION TWO

Harbours, Streets and Buildings

The Market Square, St Just, early 1900s. This view, which was taken outside the Wellington Hotel, shows the early motor bus that operated from Penzance railway station and a tried and tested horse-bus.

Sennen, 1908. Work is in progress on the all-important breakwater which protects this small fishing village from the ravages of the sea.

The old flour mill at Gulval, which was operated by Bazeley & Sons. In the 1950s it became a wine factory and mead was produced here.

Mousehole harbour, *c*. 1920. Today it is known throughout the world for its picturesque views and is the haunt of artists and tourists. It was once a busy fishing harbour, but nowadays the pleasure craft outnumber the working boats.

Keigwin Arms, Mousehole, 1931. At the time it operated as a café, and a sign over the door read '1s 3d Cream Tea, 1s Plain Tea'.

Washing day, Newlyn, 1906. No automatic washing machines were available then, so a tub and washboard had to suffice.

Chywoone Hill, Newlyn. This early view is difficult to date but was probably taken in the late 1880s.

Keel Alley, Newlyn, in the late 1940s. This area no longer exists because it was filled in when the new pier was constructed.

Alexandra Road, Penzance, c. 1905. This postcard was produced by the Pictorial Stationery Co. in London, but it was printed in Saxony in Germany. At the turn of the century most colour postcards were printed in Germany.

Market Jew Street, Penzance, c. 1904. This view shows the Market House, which was built in 1838, and the statue commemorating Penzance's famous son, Sir Humphry Davy, who invented the safety lamp for miners.

The drawing room of Penlee House, Penzance, c. 1880. Today this room is one of the art galleries in the Penzance Museum. The Branwells, who owned the house, were one of the wealthiest families in Penwith. The house was surrounded by a park of some thirteen acres.

Another view of the drawing room in Penlee House. Before the advent of wireless and television, families had to make their own entertainment, and virtually all houses had a musical instrument, in most cases a piano. Penlee was no exception.

Wood Street and the start of the Terrace in Market Jew Street, Penzance. The street lamp was lit each night by the borough lamplighter. Two of the original lamps were saved by Penzance Museum when all the street lamps were being replaced in 1992.

Alverton, Penzance, 1908. This view shows the Western Hotel which was demolished and recently replaced by Branwell House, the local offices of the DSS. On the right are the Stewart Buildings which were then occupied by Houlson & Son, tobacconists and hairdressers. The ladies' salon was on the first floor.

The Promenade, Penzance, c. 1880. This photograph was taken from Batten and Couches Wharf, which is now the site of the Jubilee bathing pool.

The Old Look Out, Coinagehall Street, Penzance, *c.* 1890.

Penzance harbour in a photograph taken for Francis Frith & Co. Ltd in 1897. It is fortunate that this company numbered all their photographs so that dating each picture is easy.

Penzance harbour office, *c.* 1919. This was superseded by a new office and weighbridge which is used today by the Isles of Scilly Steamship Co.

Penzance harbour, *c.* 1870. These three sailing vessels have been beached, which was a common practice to make the unloading of cargoes easier.

Penzance from Newlyn, *c.* 1895. On the left is Bodilly's flour mill at Wherrytown. On the right is the Serpentine Works, which was later the site of the Bedford Bolitho Gardens.

The Battery Rocks, Penzance, *c.* 1880. In 1739 it was decided that fortifications were needed on the rocks overlooking Penzance harbour, and this photograph shows the gun house which was built at that time.

West End, Marazion, 1905. The coastguard station is on the left.

Old cottages, Marazion, c. 1905. Today thatched cottages are very rare in Penwith, but at the turn of the century thatch was one of the most common roofing materials.

Marazion, 1919. The building on the left is the town hall and fire station. The area that was occupied by the fire station now houses the town's museum, which opened in 1992.

The Square, Marazion, 1919. This view has not changed much over the years except for the hoards of visitors that now stop at Marazion on their way to St Michael's Mount.

Turnpike Hill, Marazion, 1919. The horses were possibly on their way to the town's farrier in Shop Hill.

Marazion from St Michael's Mount, c. 1880. The structure in the foreground is a lighthouse, the 'Light of St Michael'. It was first referred to in 1433 when a sum of money was left for its upkeep by Sir John Arundell.

St Michael's Mount from Marazion, 1890.

Chevy Chase Room, St Michael's Mount, 1908. The room gains its name from the frieze that runs around its walls.

St Michael's Mount, 1895. The conical building on the left was the Mount's dairy and just to the right can be seen the disturbed ground that delineates the route of the underground railway which runs from the harbour to the castle.

The folly near Castle-an-Dinas quarry. Today it is in an even more ruinous state.

Madron Workhouse or Penzance Union, *c.* 1965. Built in 1839, it saw its share of pitiful life stories. The photograph shows the derelict building shortly before its demolition when the grounds were used as a general tip.

Porthcurno valley, 1892. The valley was the site of one of the earliest experiments in submarine telegraphy. The first cable was laid into the cove in 1870, and it was quickly followed by cables that connected Britain with all of its empire. Until recently Cable and Wireless plc, a direct descendant of the company that laid the first cable, maintained a training college in the valley.

Lamorna valley, photographed by James Valentine in around 1890.

Bosava Mill, Lamorna, photographed by Gibson and Sons of Penzance in around 1880.

Treen valley, *c.* 1930. This view is taken from a sepia postcard that was produced by R. Williams, Fancy Goods Depot, Penzance.

Ludgvan, *c.* 1880. This rare postcard was found in the Richard Angove collection which was bequeathed to the Penzance library on his recent death.

Roundhouse, Sancreed, *c.* 1890. It is said that the walls were built with no corners so

that the devil could not sit inside.

Crowlas at the turn of the century. The Star Inn had recently been built. In those days it was still quite a novelty to have your photograph taken – people seem to be peering out from every door and window.

This view of Crowlas, looking towards Penzance, was probably taken at the same time as the previous photograph.

Crowlas, *c.* 1890. The cyclist seems to be bored with having his photograph taken or he has found something extremely interesting in his newspaper.

The original Longship lighthouse at the Land's End, *c.* 1870. Built in 1795, it lasted until 1873 when it was replaced by the present tower.

Pendeen lighthouse, *c.* 1905.

Godrevy lighthouse, 1890. It was built in 1858 following the wreck of the *Nile* on 12 December 1854. It was immortalized in Virginia Woolf's novel *To the Lighthouse*, which she wrote while living in St Ives.

St Ives harbour from an engraving dated 1842. There is a lot of artistic licence in this view, but this was not uncommon in engravings of the period.

Porthminster, St Ives, *c.* 1900. The buildings at the top right are the coastguards' houses.

St Ives harbour, 1884. These two panoramic views show the harbour on the same day at

different states of the tide.

Valley Road, Carbis Bay, *c.* 1950. This view, looking towards Hayle, shows many areas of land which had yet to see development.

Lelant, *c.* 1918. The Lelant Hotel is known today as The Badger Inn. This is a tranquil scene, and there isn't a motor car in sight.

Hayle, from Lelant Ferry, *c.* 1900. Even then the silting of the estuary was a problem – a vessel seems to be stuck on the bar.

Hayle harbour, *c.* 1890. Hayle was in its heyday then. Engines from here were supplied to mines throughout the world and they were used to drain the meres in Holland, and Harvey and Co. were building ships and all manner of other machinery.

Hayle, July 1956. In the foreground is the works of the Associated Ethyl Co. Ltd, while

in the background is the power station. Both have since been demolished.

The Plantation, Hayle, *c.* 1906. This tree-lined walk still exists and a pleasant evening stroll is still possible.

Hayle Terrace and St Elwyn's church, *c.* 1905. This postcard was published by E. Williams of the ARK in Hayle, a business that is still operating in the town.

Penpol and Clifton Terraces, Hayle, *c.* 1900. The railway track on the left ran under a viaduct to sidings in the works of Harvey and Co.

Undercliff, Phillack, *c.* 1900. This view has changed considerably with recent development.

Millpond, Hayle, *c.* 1905. The area around the millpond has recently been refurbished by the Hayle Town Trust and a small open-air theatre is planned on the adjoining land.

Shops, Public Houses and Hotels

Dolphin Tavern, Penzance. This is situated on the quayside and is believed to have been a haunt of smugglers. When it was rebuilt at the turn of the century, a secret store and a passage thought to lead to the Battery Rocks were said to have been found.

The Old Inn at Madron in around 1880 when the licensee was John Michell. This rare photograph is badly damaged and has, I believe, never been published before.

The Old Inn, Gulval, *c.* 1880. This is now the site of The Coldstreamer.

Godolphin Hotel, Marazion, 1928. This is the only purpose-built hotel in Marazion.

Logan Rock Hotel, Treen. This postcard, dating from around 1890, was actually posted in 1965! I wonder if today's postcards will have such a long shelf life.

The First and Last Hotel in England, Sennen, 1908.

The Square, Hayle, *c.* 1900. In the centre is the present White Hart, while on the left is the original White Hart which was operated by Jane Trevithick, wife of Richard Trevithick.

Fore Street, Hayle, *c*. 1900. To the right can be seen the entrance to the Cornubia Hotel with its original columns which have unfortunately been replaced by square brick pillars.

The George & Dragon Inn, Market Place, St Ives, *c*. 1875.

TREGENNA CASTLE HOTEL, St. Ives, Cornwall

Telephone :
St. Ives 38.

(Under the management of the Great Western Railway Co.)

Telegrams :
"Tregotel," St. Ives
Cornwall.

Tregenna Castle Hotel, St Ives. Originally this was the home of the Stephens family. It was bought by the Great Western Railway Co. in 1877 and was converted and extended to become the most important hotel in St Ives.

The High Street at St Ives in around 1910, before the cinema was built.

Tregenna Place, St Ives, *c.* 1900. Now every summer this street throngs with tourists and their vehicles.

Market Square, St Just, *c.* 1946. This post-war view of the square was taken when rationing was still in operation.

First and Last post office in England, Sennen, *c.* 1900. At the time the post office was situated in the cove.

First and Last post office in England, Sennen, *c.* 1927. By the time this photograph was taken the post office had moved from the cove up to the main road.

SECTION FOUR

Places of Worship and Antiquity

A distant view of Perranuthnoe church, *c.* 1900. The church is dedicated to St Piran. It was rebuilt in 1842, but the tower dates from the fifteenth century.

St Hilary church, 1931. This church became famous in the 1930s when Father Bernard Walke and his wife Anne invited artists from the Newlyn colony to decorate the building. These artists included Harold Harvey and Ernest Procter. The church has the only spire in west Cornwall.

All Saints church, Marazion, 1908. The building dates from 1865.

The chapel on St Michael's Mount, 1908. St Michael's Mount is a separate parish from Marazion.

Paul church, 1908. This church has a delightful lantern on top of the tower and has the dubious accolade of having been torched by the Spaniards when they raided the bay in 1595. Fortunately all they managed to accomplish was smoke damage.

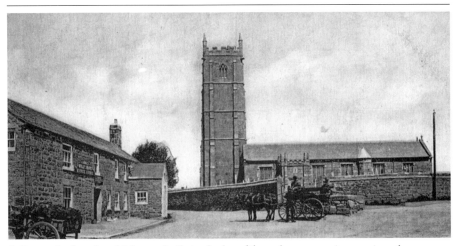

St Buryan's church, which was built in the late fifteenth century. At one time there was a deanery here.

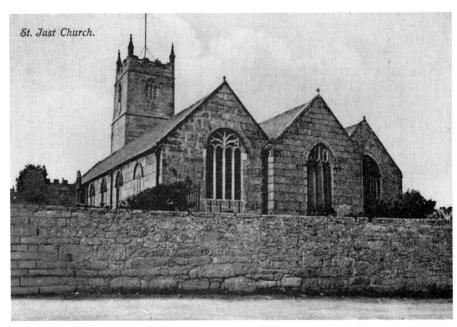

St Just church was built in the fourteenth century. This picture dates from around 1900.

Wesleyan church, St Just, *c.* 1910. This view of the interior attests to the great number of Wesleyans who lived in the town and surrounding area. Every small hamlet had its Nonconformist chapel. Today many of these buildings are derelict or have been converted into private dwellings.

Sennen church, 1931. The building dates from the thirteenth century.

This early view of Zennor shows that it was once a much larger settlement than it is

today. The church was built in around 1450.

This bench-end in Zennor church depicts the Mermaid of Zennor. There is a legend that a mermaid once sang in the church and that a young man from Zennor, Matthew Trewhella, was so entranced by her that he followed her to the sea and was never seen again. Later, when a boat anchored just off Zennor, a mermaid came to the surface and asked the captain to move because the anchor was blocking the entrance to her and Matthew's home.

St Ives church from an engraving by W. Willis, *c*. 1880. The church is dedicated to St Ia and was built around 1400.

St Elwyn's church, Hayle, *c*. 1890. This photograph was taken before the church hall was built.

A view of Phillack church in a postcard by Argall, *c*. 1900. The church was built around 1500. Until the building of St Elwyn's, Phillack was the parish church of Hayle.

The old thatched chapel at Gwithian.

Gwithian church, *c.* 1900. This view was obviously used as a Christmas card. The church was rebuilt in 1865 and it is dedicated to St Gothan.

St Gothan's oratory, Gwithian, *c.* 1880. This ruin is also known as the 'buried church'.

Chapel Carn Brea, Sancreed, *c.* 1880

Penzance Natural History and Antiquarian Society at the Men-An-Tol, 1907. The society went to a number of ancient sites during its annual tour. The Men-An-Tol has

recently been found to be part of a large stone circle.

The Pipers. Between 1 and 22 August 1928 two women visited Penwith, and they kept an accurate diary of their tour. The next six photographs come from their album. The relevant entry in the diary reads: 'Sunday the 5th, Charabanc to St Buryan; left charabanc thence by a field path to a Menhir standing in the hedge, thence to one of the Pipers.'

Chun Quoit. 'The quoit examined by W.C. Borlase, 1871: the barrow or cairn which originally enclosed the dolmen still reached in some places nearly to the top of the supporter. Diameter of the mound 32 ft.'

Zennor Quoit. 'Bus to Gurnards Head Hotel . . . to Zennor Quoit . . . In 1750 [according to] Dr William Borlase Rector of Ludgvan (1695–1772) [the quoit was wrecked] by a farmer to obtain stone for cattle shelter.'

Mulfra Quoit. 'Onto Mulfra Hill: old mine shafts: Mulfra Quoit and several barrows. Dr W. Borlase made an excavation under the Quoit but found only some layers of clay – black, white and yellow. Return to Newmill.'

Chysauster Fogou, Tuesday 6 August 1928. 'The cave, giants' cavern or fogou runs in several yards but is probably not now complete.' This fogou was filled in quite recently by English Heritage despite offers by local archaeologists to make it safe.

Lanyon Quoit, Saturday 4 August 1928. 'Bus to Madron . . . thence to Lanyon Quoit, the cavity of this dolmen had been dug out before the time of Dr W. Borlase: no relics preserved: structure fell in 1815: originally 4 uprights: re-erected 1824 but uprights reduced in height.'

SECTION FIVE

Entertainment, Celebration and Disaster

St Just carnival, *c.* 1920. The annual carnival in many a Penwith town was, and still is, a time of great jollity.

Quay Fair by J.G. Moyle. This painting depicts the Midsummer's Day fair, which was held as part of St John's feast. The building on the right is the Dolphin Tavern which is also pictured on page 53.

Children with May horns in the Coombe, Newlyn, *c*. 1915. The custom was to blow these horns early on May Day morning. This was eventually banned in the Borough of Penzance, so children used to go just outside the borough's boundary and blow the horns there.

Circus elephants parade through Chapel Street, Penzance, c. 1907. The elephants used to have a daily bath in the harbour while the show was in town.

Another part of the circus parade, Chapel Street, Penzance, c. 1907.

Henry Jones's annual fair at Halsetown. The fair was set up in a field. Three of the showman's engines can be seen mingling with the vegetables, and in the background is what appears to be an ancient Ford or Morris commercial van. The Jones family came to Halsetown from the late nineteenth century to the 1930s, when this photograph was taken.

Corpus Christi fair, Penzance, c. 1925. This was the largest such fair in Cornwall. Seen in the foreground are Anderton and Rowland's three engines – *Dragon*, *Earl Beatty* and *Lion* – which generated power for the scenic railway.

The Minack Theatre, *c*. 1950. First opened in the 1930s by Rowena Cade, today it is visited by many thousands of people every season.

Shakespeare festival, Penwith, 1950s. The annual festival had its origins in a similar pre-war event.

The unveiling of the Boer War memorial in Morrab Gardens by the Mayoress of Penzance on 5 November 1904.

A march past of the 2nd Duke of Cornwall Light Infantry, c. 1900. On the arch are the names of some of the campaigns in which the regiment took part, including Egypt (1882) the Nile (1884) and Lucknow.

The 2nd Duke of Cornwall Light Infantry marching down Market Jew Street, *c.* 1900.

Triumphal arch at Wherrytown, Penzance. It was erected at the end of the First World War.

The great blizzard of March 1891. These men are trying to clear the road from Heamoor to Madron.

The Bay of Panama which was wrecked during the great blizzard of 1891. She foundered under the cliffs just south of Nare Point on the Lizard peninsula. Although this is not a Penwith photograph, it graphically shows another aspect of the severity of the blizzard. It is said that men were frozen on the rigging.

Ornais II wrecked on 6 December 1929, near Perran.

HMS *Warspite* went aground at Mount Mopus ledge near Cudden Point on 19 April 1947. The ship was later towed to St Michael's Mount where it was broken up between 1947 and 1952.

Lady of the Isles struck a rock while out on an evening pleasure cruise in 1903 and was purposely run aground at Lamorna. The ship was built at Harveys of Hayle and operated on the Penzance to Isles of Scilly route.

Falmouth Castle wrecked at Porthcurno.

City of Cardiff wrecked at the Land's End. A breeches buoy is in operation between the vessel and the shore.

Submarine L1 wrecked at Cape Cornwall on 29 March 1930.

Flowergate wrecked off Porthminster beach, St Ives, 1946.

HMS *Wave* broke loose and ran aground at St Ives between the harbour and Porth-minster beach on 2 October 1952.

Caroline Parsons, St Ives's first motor lifeboat, was wrecked on the Island at St Ives while rescuing the crew of the Panamanian vessel SS *Alba* on 31 January 1938.

Romeo aground on Hayle bar, 22 December 1971. This bar has been the cause of numerous wrecks and groundings. Harveys operated a number of sluice pools that were designed to scour out the shipping channel and alleviate such problems.

The Land's End and Tourism

The First and Last refreshment room in England, *c.* 1880. The establishment was run by Grace Thomas.

A much-extended First and Last refreshment room, with the Longship lighthouse in the distance. The photograph was taken by Francis Frith in 1927.

The Penwith House Temperance Hotel, 1908.

The Temperance Hotel in 1927, with a number of tourists milling around the headland.

The Land's End Hotel, 1927. Recent developments have considerably altered the appearance of the hotel.

The Land's End Hotel, 1928. Many people think that erosion is a modern problem, but even then it was a constant worry.

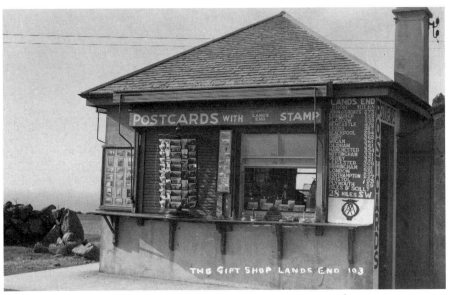

Gift shop, the Land's End. From this little shop many thousands of postcards were sold, all bearing the special postmark 'Land's End'.

A group visiting the Land's End, *c*. 1910. This vehicle was operated by the Great Western Railway.

Motorcycles preparing for the off outside the Land's End Hotel, *c*. 1908.

Two early motor vehicles outside the Land's End Hotel, *c.* 1908.

S. Jacka's Temperance House, Logan Rock, *c.* 1905.

St. Ives.

We have discovered a sweet little cove near here.

A postcard dating from around 1914, extolling the virtues of St Ives.

St. Ives Bay.   JW&S 241

One more for your collection A. P.

Porthminster beach, St Ives, *c.* 1902. At this time only the address was allowed on the back of a postcard so any writing had to go on the front!

Entrance to Thicket, St. Ives   My time has been very pleasantly
                                              filled in here

A comic postcard which was probably used at many different resorts; the town's name was the only thing that changed.

Hayle Towans showing Knill's Steeple and St Ives, 1927.

Hayle Towans in the 1950s. This view shows the development that occurred in the twenty-five years that separate this photograph from the one above.

Paddling pool at Hayle Towans, *c.* 1925. Pools such as this are regularly scoured out by the tide.

Gwithian beach, looking towards Hayle, *c.* 1950.

Looking towards Hayle from Godrevy, *c. 1950*. This photograph was taken by Garfield Hall for Penzance Borough Council and was included in its tourist guide.

This postcard with its views of the Esplanade at Penzance and Logan Rock was produced around 1910. The message on the reverse thanks Miss Mabel Jenkins of Veronica Cottage, Bryher, Isles of Scilly, for sending some flowers.

The Promenade, Penzance, *c*. 1910.

Morrab Gardens, Penzance, *c*. 1912. A concert is in progress.

Strolling on the Promenade at Penzance, which was the centre of attraction for all visitors to the town. The Queen's Hotel and the Mount's Bay Hotel are in the background of this view, which dates from 1919.

The Promenade, Penzance, 1919. On the left can be seen the Pavillion, which was opened in 1911.

Penzance's indoor swimming pool, *c*. 1880. The pool was situated on the Promenade.

Jersey cars outside Woodfield's Alexandra Serpentine Works, Penzance. They are about to leave for the Land's End and Logan Rock.

SECTION SEVEN

Fishing, Farming and Horticulture

The Fish Quay, Newlyn, Penzance, *c.* 1900. It was common practice then for boats to unload their catches directly into horsedrawn carts.

Newlyn harbour and village, *c*. 1895. Penzance is visible in the distance.

A fishwife with her basket in Market Jew Street, Penzance. These women walked throughout the district selling their fish.

Gossip, Newlyn, *c.* 1880. The fishermen and their families lived in the many courts and small streets that can still be seen in the village.

The craft of making crab pots from withies is still carried on in the area, although most of the pots used today are not made in this way.

The road to the beach, Porthgwarra, photographed in around 1880 by James Valentine.

The beach and cove at Porthgwarra, *c.* 1880. This photograph was produced by Gibson of Penzance.

Porthglaze cove, Treen, *c*. 1880. The seining station here was once a hive of activity. Today the fish cellar is all that remains.

Sennen, 1928. On the extreme right is the roundhouse which contained the capstan that pulled the boats up into the cove.

A view of Penberth cove, showing fishing boats and the necessary capstan, *c.* 1880.

Unloading a catch at Sennen cove, near the Land's End, *c.* 1880. These boats used seine nets which surrounded complete shoals.

Hevva Hevva! This painting is by Percy Craft who was one of the Newlyn school of artists. The picture shows Bunkers Hill in St Ives. The man just left of centre is the 'huer' who kept a lookout for the shoals of fish.

Tucking a School of Pilchards by Percy Craft. This painting shows the tuck boats emptying the seine net. This picture and the preceding one are part of the collection housed in Penzance Museum.

The fish market, St Ives, *c.* 1900.

St Ives harbour, *c.* 1900.

Porthminster beach and St Ives harbour. On the left are the various boats used in seine fishing.

Mount's Bay has long been known for the production of early season vegetables. Ploughmen with horses tilled the soil for thousands of years until the advent of the internal combustion engine.

Cauliflower picking in fields on the eastern side of Marazion, *c.* 1950.

The arrival of the threshing set was an important time of year for all farmers. Help was brought in from other farms and the farmers' wives often supplied homemade cider.

Eglosmeor watermill, Zennor, *c*. 1890. This mill stood below the millpool at Carn Cobba. The building was ruined when it was hit by a torrent of water 20 ft high which rushed down the Zennor valley during the great flood of November 1894.

The smithy at Buryas bridge, *c*. 1880.

E. Jenkin and Sons, blacksmiths of Madron, *c*. 1930.

Sheepshearing was a hard task before the advent of mechanical clippers.

It was common practice at the turn of the century for many householders, large and small, to keep a pig in their back yard. At an appropriate time the pig would be killed and most of the meat preserved in saltpetre.

Before the invention of the mechanical milking machine, many farms had milkmaids who milked the cows twice a day.

Flower girls packing daffodils in a former artist's studio at Lamorna, 1938.

Knee-deep in flowers, 1938. Pickers gathering Scilly whites at Boskenna.

Autumn glory, *c.* 1935.

Mining and Quarrying

Levant mine, *c.* 1900.

Levant mine, *c*. 1900. The engine house on the left contains the beam engine that has recently been restored by the Trevithick Society and the National Trust.

The Man Engine shaft at the Levant mine. This was where the 1919 disaster, which cost the lives of thirty-one miners, began.

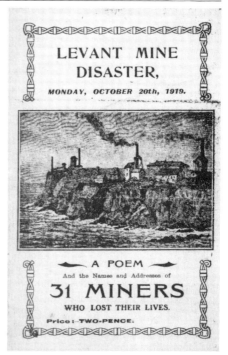

LEVANT MINE DISASTER,

MONDAY, OCTOBER 20th, 1919.

A POEM

And the Names and Addresses of

31 MINERS

WHO LOST THEIR LIVES.

Price: TWO-PENCE.

The front cover of a leaflet that was produced to raise money for the families of miners killed in the 1919 Levant mine disaster, the second worst accident in the history of Cornish mining. The Man Engine, which was first used in 1856, collapsed and thirty-one men were killed when the pin fixing the rod to the beam broke.

Waiting for news of the Levant mine disaster, 20 October 1919.

Lines on the Disaster.

St. Just, Pendeen, and Neighbourhood
  Will never forget the day
When thirty-one poor Miners
  Were suddenly called away.

This fearful accident occurred,
  On Monday at Levant,
And many a home is fatherless
  Through this terrible event.

The Man Engine was at fault, they say;
  Whilst bearing human freight,
Though very near the surface, smashed
  And sent them to their fate.

The awful strenuous hours that passed,
  Whilst bringing up the dead
And rescuing the wounded,
  The thought we almost dread.

There were many willing helpers
  Came over from Geevor Mine,
To help the rescuing parties,
  Which was merciful and kind.

The Doctors, too, must have our thanks
  For attentiveness and skill,
In succouring wounded comrades
  Brought to surface very ill.

The Parson and the Minister
  Both rendered yeoman aid,
To alleviate the sufferers,
  Christian diligence displayed.

Now in conclusion let me say
  To rich as well as poor—
Remember the Widows and Orphans
  Of those that's gone before.

K. A.

Inside cover of the fundraising leaflet.

A body has just been brought to the surface and is about to be taken to the mortuary.

Assembling for the inquest at Levant.

A list of the dead from the fundraising
leaflet.

131

Tin streamers in the Kenidjack valley, St Just, 1922.

A nineteenth-century engraving of Botallack mine.

Botallack mine, *c*. 1865. The workings extended over 2,500 ft under the sea. The mine was visited by Queen Victoria in 1846 and the Prince and Princess of Wales in 1865.

The horsedrawn whim or winding drum at Geevor mine, *c*. 1885.

Geevor mine, showing the aerial ropeway.

Geevor miners, *c*. 1920.

A painting of a flooded clay pit at Nancledra by Herbert Truman. China clay was quarried at a number of sites in the Penwith area, although it is more usually associated with the St Austell region.

Lamorna quarry in an engraving by R.T. Pentreath, *c.* 1860.

Lamorna cove and quarry, *c.* 1900.

SECTION NINE
Transport

An engraving of Penzance from the sea by R.T. Pentreath, *c.* 1860.

Landing on the Wolf Rock lighthouse. The entry to the tower is 40 ft up. In the background is the Trinity House vessel *Satellite*.

Men pulling the St Ives lifeboat *Caroline Parsons* down to the water.

The *Lyonesse*, built in Hayle by Harvey and Co., operated on the Penzance to Isles of Scilly route.

Loading cattle onto the *Lyonesse*.

Donkey carts were used for all manner of purposes, from general haulage to carrying fish.

The *Victoria*, which operated on the route between Penzance and the Land's End, *c.* 1880.

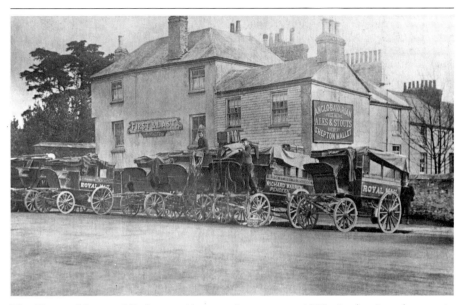

The First and Last public house, Alverton, Penzance, *c.* 1880. At the time the area in front of the building was Penzance's bus station.

The *Express*, seen here leaving Penzance in around 1880, operated on the Penzance–Helston–Falmouth route.

The Penzance steam fire engine, donated to the town by the Bolitho family.

Ready for action: the fire engine is seen here alongside St John's Hall on the day it was presented to the town.

A fire-fighting demonstration in progress outside the Queen's Hotel on the Promenade, Penzance. Note the use of a canvas water tank.

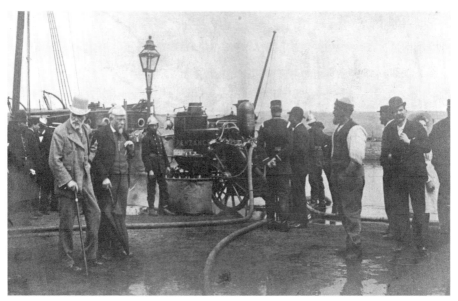

Another demonstration on presentation day, this time on Wharf Road by the harbour.

Harvey and Co. produced a large steam engine for the Dutch government to drain one of Holland's meres for land reclamation. When the cylinder was checked it was found to be substandard and for years it stood by the main road in Hayle.

Levant mine's Aveling and Porter traction engine, seen here delivering a boiler to the mine's power house.

Levant mine's Fowler road locomotive, pulling a road train. These were usually loaded with coal or ore.

The first motor car in Penzance, seen here with a crowd of onlookers.

A Milnes-Daimler 20 hp bus, operated by the Great Western Railway, outside the Commercial Hotel, St Just. The livery was chocolate and red.

The first Great Western Railway bus on the St Just route. The open compartment behind the driver was used for mail and, when empty, for smokers.

The first double-decker bus run by the Great Western Railway, 1904. It ran between Marazion and Newlyn via Penzance.

The staff outing of Messrs Genatosan Ltd to Newquay, 2 September 1919. The picture
was taken outside the offices of Trelawny Motors on the Promenade at Penzance.

A bus belonging to Hawkeys Tours on the road to the Land's End, *c.* 1950.

A Rover on the road to St Just, with Zennor in the background, *c*. 1950.

Hill climb at Trengwainton, Madron. The sport was popular in the 1950s.

Another hill climb at Trengwainton.

Motorcycle racing was also staged at Trengwainton, Madron.

A de Havilland Rapide taking off from the Land's End aerodrome.

The end of an era: the day helicopters took over on the Scillies route, 1964.

Once the Rapides were no longer in service on the Scillies route, they were used to give scenic flights.

A 'County' class locomotive, seen here at Hayle, pulling the 'down' night sleeper, *c.* 1955.

The viaduct at Hayle with a 'down' train to Penzance, *c.* 1955.

A broad-gauge tank locomotive in Penzance station, *c.* 1880.

An early view of Penzance station, *c.* 1870.

The locomotive *Penzance* at the first Penzance shed, which was just outside the station, *c.* 1900.

Long Rock sheds, Penzance, *c*. 1950.

Pyrland Hall at Penzance shed, August 1945.

No. 4509, a 2–6–2T locomotive, at Penzance shed in August 1945. These stalwart little engines were used on the St Ives and Helston branch lines.

Arlington Grange at Penzance shed, August 1945.

The last steam train to enter Penzance, 3 May 1964.

Janner's train pulled quarry trains from Penlee to the stone quay at Newlyn. The train was named after the driver, and the locomotive was built in Germany.

Acknowledgements

The photographs come from the collections of Penzance & District Museum & Art Gallery, Penzance Town Council, Penzance (Subscription) Library and their Angove collection. I should like to thank Dr Eric Richards, who did much of the initial cataloguing of the Penzance Museum's photographic collection, and I should mention the photographers themselves, Gibson, Preston, Richards, Frith, Valentine, Penhaul and the many others who did not put their names to their work.